## DEFENSIVE ARMS

Two types of arms, in general, are adopted in this exercise: offensive & defensive. The defensive mainly serve simply to cover the body: the collar, breastplate, backplate, armlet, helmet, and gauntlet. Armor from the belt down is not used (although sometimes in Germany



that the ladies most admire, which is composure, and lightness on one's feet, which is also an indication of nobility of spirit.

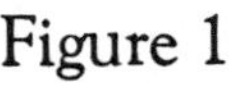

Figure 1

## HOW TO CARRY THE WAR PIKE ON THE SHOULDER WHILE CROSSING THE FIELD

The knight's visor is up to show his first action, surveying the field. He inclines the war pike over his shoulder, the fingers of his right hand forward near the butt, thumb pointing to the rear. The butt is in line with the right leg, the pike head a little higher than the butt. He holds his elbow below shoulder level, and the hand is positioned to allow a comfortable bend at the elbow. The knight positions his thumb to allow for ease of operation and grace.

## OFFENSIVE ARMS

The offensive arms are mainly swords, pikes, and axes. The war pike serves only for the pageant, and every knight must provide it himself. It is ordinarily fifteen feet long. It has a pointed head of iron (real or imitation). Almost at the center of the pike, there is a sheath of velvet, or other colored fabric, with fringes of gold, or silver, or silk, which covers the shaft for about an arm's length. The half pike serves for the barriers, and battle, and is usually provided by the field, that is by the challenger. It should be six to seven arm lengths in measure, made of light wood, and very dry, so as not to bend, but to break easily.

Figure 2

## A DIFFERENT WAY TO CARRY THE WAR PIKE

The knight may carry it with the right hand, at the side, pike head forward, elbow behind. He may want to alternate this hold with that shown in Fig. 1. He may hold the half pike at his side as well. Often, he will raise the pike to shoulder level as he strides with his right foot, lowering the pike as he strides with his left, observing the drum beat.

## THE DRUMMER

The drummer must be a person of spirit, vivacious, practical, and expert; and must know how to drum according to the style of all the nations, and know all the songs necessary in a war.

Figure 3

HOW TO GRASP A PIKE LEANING AGAINST A WALL OR THE SIDE OF THE PAVILION

The rule is that whichever foot is handiest when the knight approaches the pike should be placed against the butt, so that when he brings the head into his line of vision, the butt will not slip along the ground, which would not look good, and besides would force the man to use his left hand, which must not leave the sword.

Figure 4

## HOW THE KNIGHT MUST HALT WITH THE PIKE PLANTED IN THE GROUND (ORDERED)

There are two ways to do this: with the body held over the left foot, as in this figure, or over the right, as in Fig. 2; the first is Spanish, the second French in manner. According to this figure, the body is straight, suspended over the left foot, which points left. The stance is natural, not forced. The butt is as far from the right foot as that foot is from the left. The right foot points at the butt, while the right heel is directed toward the left inner ankle.

Figure 5

## HOW TO WALK WITH THE PIKE ORDERED

A knight, finding himself in the posture shown in Fig. 4, and wishing to march, starts with the right foot, since it is easier and allows the pike to do its work; that is to protect the body. On the occasion of this march, however, where certain fighters seek to demonstrate bravura, the left foot could be lifted first, if this is done in a spirited motion, lifting at the same time the whole body with a quick movement over the right leg, which afterward moves with the pike.

Figure 6

## FOLLOWING THE MARCH WITH THE PIKE ORDERED

Here one sees the continuation of the stride with the left foot: the body flanks, neither the hand nor the thumb leaves its position, and the elbow retracts so that the pike remains straight. The stance is serious, but not forced, and the left hand never leaves the sword.

Figure 7

RESHOULDERING THE WAR PIKE

This requires three actions: lifting the pike, as we see here, sliding the right hand to the middle, and placing it on the shoulder. These actions the knight may accomplish without changing stance, as one often sees among soldiers, but mainly one sees them accompanied by some different movement. The present motion is usually performed while putting the left foot forward, and placing the left hand near the right; this motion will also be employed in reordering the pike.

Figure 8

THE NEXT ACTION IN SHOULDERING THE PIKE

Here the knight puts his right hand toward the middle of the pike; he does not move the left hand, and the body always flanks.

Figure 9

THE PIKE SHOULDERED

Fig. 1 shows how to hold the war pike on the shoulder. If it were the barrier pike, the knight would hold his elbow at shoulder height. The right hand is two-thirds of the length of the pike away from the pike head.

Figure 10

## HOW TO ORDER THE PIKE

The knight uses the same three motions to plant the pike in the ground that he used to put it on his shoulder, in reverse. After he stops the butt on the ground, he releases the left hand and poses as in this figure, or as the occasion requires or according to his own whim. If he wants to turn to the right to honor princes or others, in planting the pike he should place the butt outside the right foot next to the ankle, then turn, using the left foot.

Figure 11

ANOTHER WAY TO HOLD THE ORDERED PIKE

Whereas in Fig. 4 we saw the body suspended over the left foot, the right hand at shoulder level, and the points of the feet and the butt forming a straight line, here we see the body over the right foot, the right hand grasping the pike higher up (so that the index finger is level with the top of the visor), and the feet and pike forming an obtuse triangle.

Figure 12

HOW TO MARCH WITH THE PIKE ORDERED AS IN FIGURE 11

The knight starts to march with the left foot as he moves the pike, in the style of French soldiers. He might also accompany the stride of the right foot with the pike, but reason dictates that it always precedes the body.

Figure 13

CONTINUING THE MARCH WITH THE ORDERED PIKE

We see that the pike always accompanies the left foot. The elbow bends at shoulder level, so that the lance remains straight, and the body flanks somewhat. Ordinarily, one carries the lance so that the butt traces a straight line; but for a more graceful movement, one may direct the arm to trace a half circle, here marked "A." This rule may also be observed while marching in the Spanish manner, as in Figs. 5 and 6. The raising and lowering of the pike must always be accompanied by the raising and lowering of the foot.

Figure 14

## HOW TO LIFT THE PIKE TO CARRY IT

It sometimes happens that, having finished the march across the field, the soldiers stop, take the pike, and go before the Master of the Field. First, they lift the pike as in the figure; second, they grasp the shaft with the right hand near the butt, without raising or lowering it; third, they hold the pike with the right hand only, and go to their place with a stride certainly grave, but more than anything else solicitous. They follow these steps in reverse when replanting the pike, using both hands for the war pike, the right only for the barrier pike.

Figure 15

HOW TO HOLD THE PIKE FOR REVIEW

The butt should be held about half an arm's length from the ground, always outside the right leg, so that it does not impede the march. The index finger is extended down the shaft, and the hand is turned, as much for grace as to better hold the pike.

Figure 16

HOW TO LIFT THE PIKE AND CARRY IT WHILE CONVENING IN A TROOP

The knight lifts the pike with the left hand while lifting the right at the same time, and the right hand supports the base of the butt.

Figure 17

## HOW TO CARRY THE PIKE IN A TROOP

The knight grasps the pike by the butt with the right hand. If it is the war pike, he rests it on the point of his shoulder. If it is the barrier pike, he holds it so it passes straight through the bend of his elbow.

Figure 18

## HOW TO HOLD THE PIKE BY ITS HEAD

It could happen that the knights go out into grottoes, or low, narrow places, thick woods, or shadowy hills, where they are forced to drag the pike along the ground. In this case, it should be grasped near its head, so that the thumb almost touches it. The hand rests against the side of the body, both for grace and to avoid fatigue. The left hand never leaves the sword.

Figure 19

## HOW TO REORDER THE PIKE AFTER DRAGGING IT

As soon as he enters the field, after glancing over it all, the knight should thrust forward his right hand, still holding the pike near the point, and with his left hand take it lower on the shaft, then with the right still lower, continuing until the right is in place to be at shoulder height once the pike is ordered. Some like to perform this action with the right hand only; but because the shaft could slip from the hand, and because this method does not conform to military standards, I do not like it.

Figure 20

## MORE ABOUT REGATHERING THE PIKE AFTER DRAGGING IT

This figure shows how to go about taking up the pike until the knight grasps the butt end, orders it, or holds it in an offensive action. The knight must not move from the stance shown here, with the left foot in front, until he is ready to order the pike, when he should draw the left foot near the right in proper position.

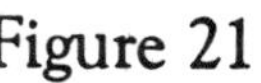

Figure 21

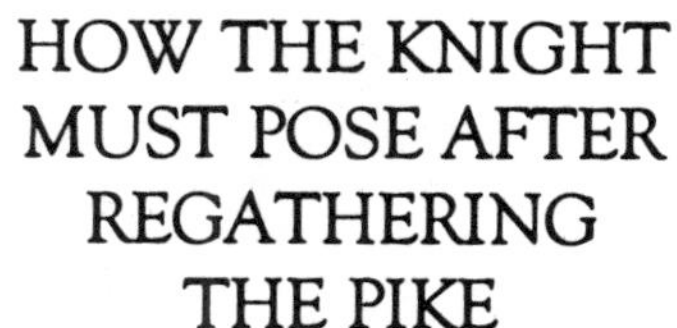

## HOW THE KNIGHT MUST POSE AFTER REGATHERING THE PIKE

Although this shows the first position for the knight to assume after taking up the pike and replacing it, this pose also serves the *padrino*, or second, when he holds the pike in order to present it to the knight when he goes to fight. The right hand grasps the war pike at shoulder level; with the barrier pike, since it is a half pike, the same hand grasps it at chest level, as one sees here.

## THE ANTIQUITY OF THE SECOND

That the use of seconds is ancient is attested by Homer in the account of the combat between Paris and Menelaus, who had as his second Ulysses, the wisest and most astute knight who yet has lived, and unique in counsels of war; and the other had Hector, the first in those times in the art of war, and not of a yielding spirit to anyone in valor, nor in strength.

Figure 22

## HOW THE KNIGHT MUST STAND WHILE AWAITING THE PIKE BEFORE ENTRY INTO BATTLE

A knight may use different methods when entering the palisade for combat. First, he may have the war pike in hand, and when the time comes, this is taken from him, and the one for combat given to him by the *padrino*. Second, he may enter with the barrier pike. Third, he may have no arms, as shown here. The first two modes are the custom in war; the third, the style of the duel. When he presents himself in the arena, the knight has his visor open; once the arms are approved, the second closes it for him. While the knight waits for his arms, he should not stand motionless, but instead pose with his body now over one foot, now over the other, so that he will always show a certain readiness and spirit of desire for combat.

Figure 23

## HOW THE SECOND SHOULD GIVE THE PIKE TO THE KNIGHT, AND HOW HE SHOULD GRASP IT

Here the pike is presented ordered. The second stands to the right of the knight, and slightly in front, and presents the pike with his right hand. He holds it a little below the place where the knight must grasp it. He is advised to offer it in such a way, with such directness towards the hand, that the knight may not err in grasping it. It is then a matter of choice whether the knight takes it with his right or left hand. Whichever he chooses, he should make a lively sweep with his arm, which signals bravura. He is advised to accompany this motion with one of his feet, whichever is more comfortable.

Figure 24

## ANOTHER WAY TO PRESENT THE PIKE

Here the second presents the pike with his right hand, holding it half an arm's length from the butt. He extends his arm almost into the line of vision of the knight, who takes the weapon with his left hand, sweeping his arm up and lifting his foot at the same time, so that when the hand joins with the shaft, the body flanks, as shown here. The sweep of the arm and lifting of the foot should be done with swiftness, spiritedness, and bravura combined to give vitality to the action. The knight is also advised to grasp the pike a little above the hand of the *padrino*.

Figure 25

WHAT THE KNIGHT MUST DO AFTER TAKING THE PIKE

Having received the pike from the second, and finding it grasped in his left hand about an arm's length from the butt end, the knight must then take this end with the right hand. In order to do this with a spirited action, he should sweep his right arm up while lifting his right foot from the ground, although the figure does not show the second movement.

Figure 26

## HOW THE KNIGHT MUST GRASP THE BUTT OF THE PIKE

In order to grip the pike at the butt end with the right hand (while it is held in the left), one may proceed freely to seize it, taking a step forward with the right foot, coming without restraint to a show of arms or a bearing of the chest. This works well if the left hand is near the butt end when the knight comes to take it with the right, but if it is far from it, as here, the knight, not being able to see, may err. I thus note this rule: first find the left hand with the right, then skillfully glide it down the shaft until it reaches the base, so that one cannot mistake it. According to the first method, the pike should be held straight by the left hand; according to the second, it is held so the pike head swings forward, as shown.

Figure 27

## HOW THE KNIGHT, AFTER THE PRECEDING MOTION, SHOULD POSE FOR ACTION

Though the figure here poses over the right foot, optimally the knight would still remain over the left foot. It is necessary, however, that the body come little by little to counterbalance itself over the left, while it moves according to Fig. 26 and arrives in the posture of Fig. 27. This posture serves not only for going forward, but also (after the engagement) for the retreat; and on still other occasions, according to the knight's intention.

Figure 28

## HOW TO HOLD THE PIKE PLANTED IN THE FIST

One holds the pike in two ways: in a tight fist, or with the fingers somewhat loosened, as shown. A tight-fisted hold accompanies a firm stance. When the knight marches, or wants to move his hand from its place in order to start an action, the fingers loosen quickly and remain spread. Note that in this posture the arm is held high, extended so that the point of the index finger is even with the top of the helmet; thus the hand does not pass near the left, nor does it impede vision. Here the pike head swings forward; on other occasions one might hold it another way.

Figure 29

## A DIFFERENT WAY TO HOLD THE PIKE PLANTED IN THE FIST

The difference between this and the preceding figure is in the grip on the pike, since this figure holds the fingers closed, the other open; the reason is that this one is posing, the other acting. As soon as the knight wishes to move in order to march, or take other action, he should open his fingers as he lifts his hand. The closed-fisted hold is used in many of the figures that follow.

Figure 30

HOW TO CARRY THE PIKE, GRASPED AT THE BUTT END, OVER THE SHOULDER

Here the pike rests on the shoulder, but it may be better to rest it on the arm between the elbow and the point of the shoulder, especially when the pike is made of a light wood. The arm is held slightly bent at the elbow in either case. The hand is at waist level, so that the point is high, and swings toward the left side. This method will serve in the reconnaissance of the field; but if the pike is of heavy wood, such as ebony, the knight should grasp it a little up from the base, and hold his arm closer in. The knight may present himself in the posture shown here inside the palisade, and may enter into many other displays from this one, as it pleases him.

Figure 31

## HOW TO MARCH WITH THE PIKE PLANTED IN THE FIST

Here and in the following figure, we see how to hold the weapon and accompany it with the stride in order to march well. When the left foot is lifted, the arm is extended; when the right is lifted, the hand retracts near the left shoulder, so that the foot which is on the ground serves always as a base for the pike. The arm is extended so that the hand is in line with the right ear.

Figure 32

CONTINUING THE MARCH WITH THE PIKE PLANTED IN THE FIST

Here we see the placement of the hand when the right foot is lifted off the ground. The hand is near the left shoulder, a good palm's length from it. The fingers are held so they appear to be open, and the index finger is spread more than the others. The body flanks slightly to the left-hand side, though the Spanish prefer to stay centered. Many like the head of the weapon to swing to the left side; others prefer it to remain straight and in line with the head; and I say the same. I could offer many reasons, but will say only that, so that the head will not shake with the sweeping motion of the arm, the weapon must be held straight and near to the head. Some like the pike to shake, but I will not praise this, since it could easily break because of this action.

Figure 33

PROPER POSTURE WITH THE PIKE PLANTED IN THE GROUND

This figure, with many others that follow, I will name Postures, because they find the knight posing with both feet on the ground, standing firm with arms motionless, ready to act according to his will. If in this posture the right hand were a little higher, on par with the top of the helmet, it would perhaps make a grander appearance. This serves as a pose for the knight (after having received the pike from the second inside the palisade) who has determined to stop and make a display with his weapon. It is a comfortable posture for making a show of respect, either from the right side or the left; though it appears that the body (thanks to the butt's placement between the feet) is better placed to make this display of reverence on the left side. If he wants to turn to the right, the knight should knock the butt end forward with his right foot, then take the shaft with his left hand, and turn his body to the right, to honor whomever he finds there.

Figure 34

A DIFFERENT POSTURE, WITH THE PIKE HELD AT MID-SHAFT

Carrying the pike at mid-shaft, with the butt end forward and the head behind, is useful to the knight when marching through the field and at other times, such as when he honors princes or judges. In the act of displaying such honors, he could, on lowering his arm, make the butt pass from the right or left side of his body to the opposite, and then stand firm. Once the pike is lowered, the knight may strike many other poses, with the help of the left hand.

Figure 35

## ANOTHER POSTURE WITH THE PIKE HELD AT THE BUTT END

In this posture, the pike may be held in two ways: the fingers may support the butt so that the shaft passes between thumb and arm; or the index finger and thumb may support it, which makes it much easier to control the pike. These methods serve (along with all the other postures) to vary marches, as when the knight takes in the field, stops to make a display of respect, reconnoiters the field, or when he is in the palisade. From this posture he may enter into others, according to the person's taste and the constraints of necessity.

Figure 36

ANOTHER POSTURE WITH THE PIKE PLANTED IN THE FIST

This figure shows a firm posture which serves on the occasions mentioned for previous figures, and also for facing the adversary or the crowd. The fingers are held together, and the point of the weapon leans a little in the direction of the head.

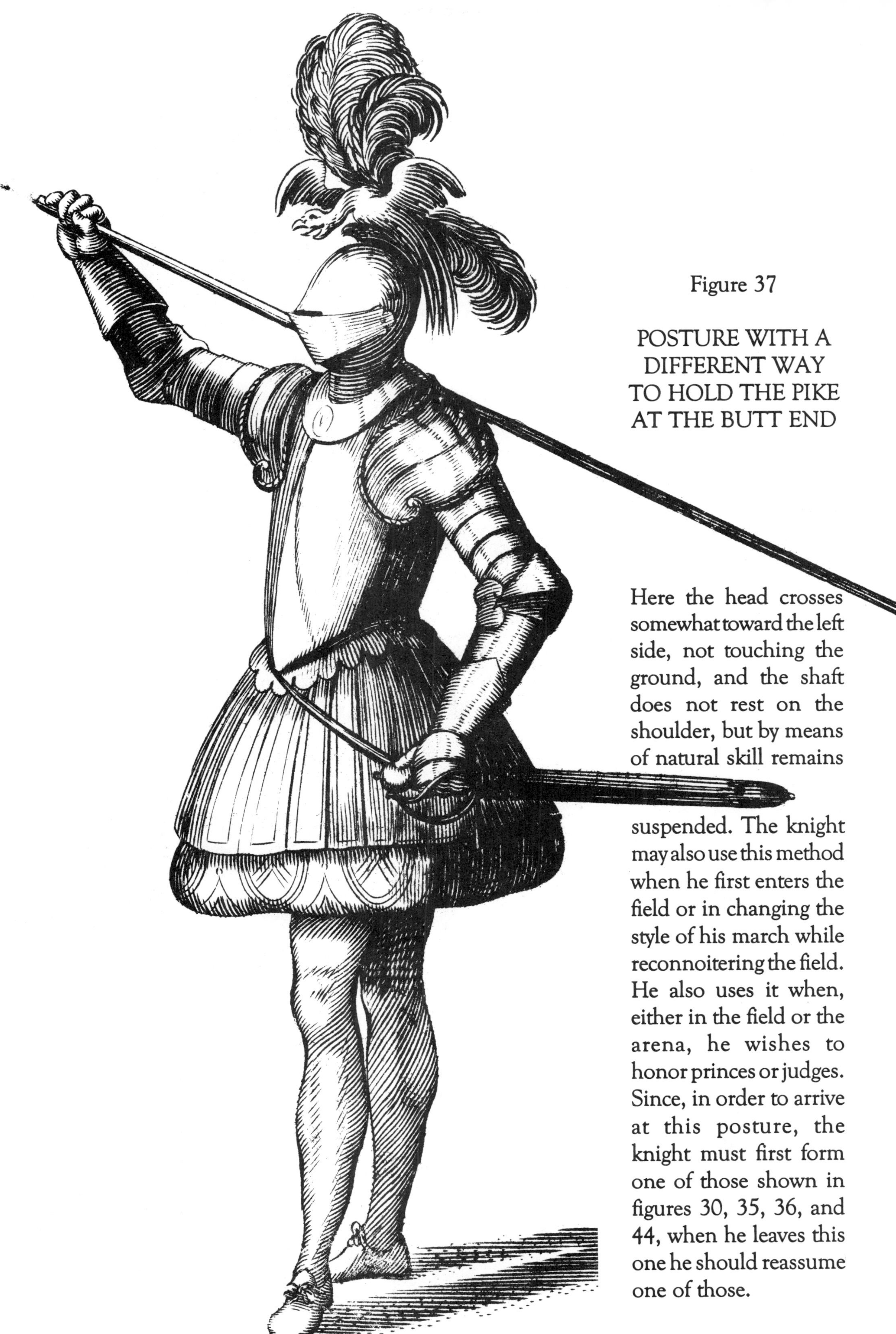

Figure 37

POSTURE WITH A DIFFERENT WAY TO HOLD THE PIKE AT THE BUTT END

Here the head crosses somewhat toward the left side, not touching the ground, and the shaft does not rest on the shoulder, but by means of natural skill remains suspended. The knight may also use this method when he first enters the field or in changing the style of his march while reconnoitering the field. He also uses it when, either in the field or the arena, he wishes to honor princes or judges. Since, in order to arrive at this posture, the knight must first form one of those shown in figures 30, 35, 36, and 44, when he leaves this one he should reassume one of those.

Figure 38

## A DIFFERENT POSTURE WITH THE PIKE GRASPED AT THE BUTT END

In this posture the knight might just as well hold his left foot forward as his right. Some prefer the arm to be extended so that the hand is even with the thigh, as a rule; but I nonetheless prefer it held a little in front, without forcing it, and somewhat beyond the thigh. In raising the pike from the ground, the knight should not push the head forward, because it would be easy to break it, but should turn his hand so the head swings right, just as he lifts his foot from the ground. Then, with a turn of the wrist, he should carry it so the head is near his left hand while he crosses the field. In order to march forward in this posture, he should lightly hit the ground with the head at each stride, carrying it forward gracefully.

Figure 39

ANOTHER POSTURE WITH THE PIKE GRASPED AT THE BUTT END

The knight, finding himself in the posture shown in Fig. 38, forms this one by lifting his arm and letting the butt of the weapon turn in his hand. He could, in order to give grace to this action, see that this hand makes a half circle as he raises his arm. Though the right foot is shown in the front here, it is more reasonable that the left foot be in front while he stands still. Among other occasions, this posture serves the knight when he stands firm in the face of the enemy.

Figure 40

HOW THE KNIGHT MUST POSE WITH THE PIKE GRASPED AT MID-SHAFT

Here, the point is forward and the butt end is behind. Finding himself in the pose shown in Fig. 27, and seizing the pike lower down the shaft, the knight will easily form the present figure. In order to do this, the left hand must grasp the weapon higher than the right, with the finger nails pointing toward the ground.

Figure 41

POSTURE WITH THE PIKE GRASPED NEAR ITS HEAD

The knight should use this posture only when he stops in front of the prince, or judges, in order to honor them inside the palisade. After this, he might (in order to display his contempt), while marching near the enemy, insert a flourish of the pike which puts him into this position, but he should not stand in it for this purpose. The more suitable figures from which to arrive at this one are 27, 28, and 29. The knight should throw the butt end forward with the right hand, letting the shaft glide through it, until he holds it as shown, accompanying this action with a step of the right foot.

Figure 42

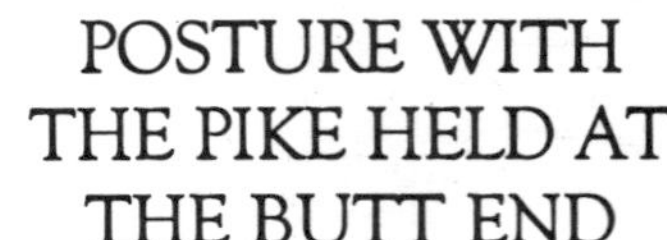

## POSTURE WITH THE PIKE HELD AT THE BUTT END

The knight might acceptably use this method of holding the barrier pike on entering the field. Similarly, while he marches on reconnaissance of the field, this posture serves for variation; and it may serve as a posture to honor the prince or judges. I would use this method of holding the pike on only two occasions: while entering the field for reconnaissance; and passing in front of the guard, once the knight is moving away from him, so that the point always is directed toward the guard.

Figure 43

## ANOTHER POSTURE WITH THE PIKE HELD NEAR ITS POINT

In this posture the butt of the pike drops behind the shoulder until it hits the ground, and the point remains high. In order to form this pose easily, the knight must begin as in Fig. 28, turning his hand a little so that the fingernails point to the sky; then, raising his arm, he will comfortably be able to make the butt end slide behind his shoulder. He could follow the same procedure from Fig. 38.

Figure 44

## POSTURE WITH THE PIKE HELD AT THE BUTT END

We see here that the pike is held totally on the right side, and the head touches the ground. The knight may use this posture inside the palisade while facing his adversary, and again when honoring princes or judges, or when preparing other actions, as he deems best. Wanting to raise the head into the air, he could observe the same rules put forward in Fig. 38. From there he might proceed to Fig. 45, or others, as he pleases.

## THE MEANING OF JUDGE

The name judge is given to those who know how to choose one thing alone from among many. They choose that side which the spirit of reason craves.... They are able to discern justice from injustice, the useful from the harmful, the good from the bad, and they know how to adjust according to the time, place, and occasion. One judge would be enough, since a multitude of judges causes irresolution; but to throw out suspicion of partiality, even though only noble and magnanimous persons are elected, nevertheless it is customary to have no fewer than three, and if more, always an odd number, so that the judgment is decided by a majority.

Figure 45

## POSTURE WITH THE PIKE ORDERED

This posture is no different from that shown in Fig. 11, save that here the hand grasps the pike higher up, and the butt end is next to the outside of the right foot. Since this posture serves the knight in the same ways and on similar occasions as that one, and also as Fig. 4, for the sake of brevity I will say no more at present regarding this one.

Figure 46

MARCH WITH THE PIKE

The knight, after having honored the princes and judges, turns to the enemy, and in order to display his skill with his arms, marches with a brief flourish of the pike to confront his adversary. The form that this proceeding may take is suggested in the present figure and in others that follow. From this figure the knight may perform different actions, according to the occasion and his will, including striking his enemy.

Figure 47

## A DIFFERENT MARCH WITH THE PIKE

The present figure demonstrates along with Fig. 48 how to form the march; this shows the forward movement of the right foot, the following the advance of the left. It is necessary to walk in a straight line while using this hold on the pike, until the knight arrives at a good distance from which to make the call to engage, or to drop the point, as in Fig. 46, and strike. Depending on the size of the field, many actions are possible.

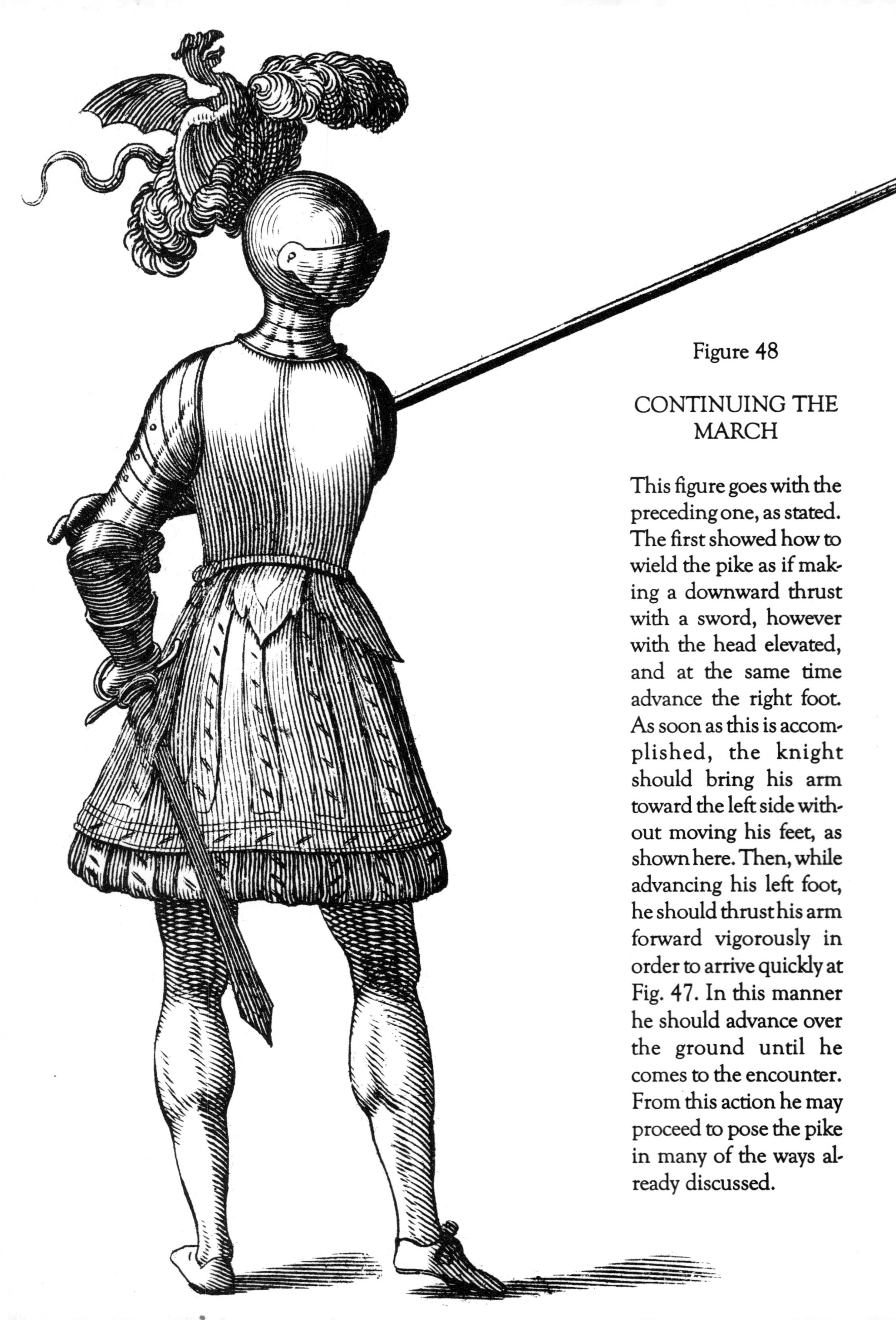

Figure 48

## CONTINUING THE MARCH

This figure goes with the preceding one, as stated. The first showed how to wield the pike as if making a downward thrust with a sword, however with the head elevated, and at the same time advance the right foot. As soon as this is accomplished, the knight should bring his arm toward the left side without moving his feet, as shown here. Then, while advancing his left foot, he should thrust his arm forward vigorously in order to arrive quickly at Fig. 47. In this manner he should advance over the ground until he comes to the encounter. From this action he may proceed to pose the pike in many of the ways already discussed.